Good News About Trouble

Good News About Trouble

by EDDY SWIESON
with Howard Norton

LOGOS INTERNATIONAL
Plainfield, New Jersey

CONTENTS

Introduction

The first words of a scribbled letter recently addressed to me carried the impact of a sharp punch in the stomach!

"To Mr. Swieson," it began, in the brisk manner of an office memo. "This morning it took me ten minutes to decide whether to stay in bed or get up and shoot myself. I'm not fooling. The gun is in my dresser drawer. By the time you read this I may have changed my mind and used it. But today I decided to give myself one more try, so I stayed in bed, where I am writing this.

"Lying here thinking what a mess I'm in I just happened to catch a few words of a speech you made on the radio. You talked about the 'zest of living.' You didn't make much sense to me, because there hasn't been any zest in my life for a long, long time. But in spite of the way I've messed up my life, I've still got enough sense to realize I don't know everything. I know that somewhere, somebody may have a secret that would make this rat race less miserable. And it struck me that you might be the one. So that's why I'm writing.

"I'm told you are into some sort of religion. Maybe you are a preacher or something. Whatever you are, you are a stranger to me, and therefore, possibly a new source of hope.

"I've tried everything else: liquor, drugs, Yoga, TM, and even hypnotism—the whole works. It all failed. And I don't think I can take one more failure, so I don't want any phony advice. If you really are on to something good, I'd like to hear about it. But it better be good. Because, if you're lying to me, remember, I have this gun. I'm going to come see you."

The letter wasn't signed, so I may never learn his or her name, or even whether this suffering human was among those I have talked to since that startling message arrived. Some of my visitors have been just as desperate and unhappy. But, to my knowledge, none carried a gun.

Experiences like this have convinced me that what this country needs is not "a good five-cent cigar" as one recent statesman proclaimed, but a good, simply written, straightforward, five-minute description of the secret of zestful living. So many are being turned in the wrong direction in their search for inner peace and happiness. If you watch television you may get the notion that you have to drink a certain brand of beer to "get your gusto." Or that you have to eat a certain brand of breakfast cereal to get you through a successful day. This is nonsense, of course. But we cannot just brush aside this Madison Avenue nonsense without putting something sensible in its place, to fill the vacuum.

That is the purpose of this little book.

The real secret of zestful living has been known for about twenty centuries. But for much of that time it has been wrapped in ponderous phrases and archaic language. And in recent years it has been so oversimplified by the excessive use of syrupy cliches, that the earnest searcher after truth has often been sickened by it, and turned elsewhere.

With these things in mind, I have asked my friend Howard Norton, a professional writer and Pulitzer Prize winner, to collaborate with me in an effort to peel away the ponderous phrases and the sickening cliches and tell it like it is, in crisp journalistic style, tailored to assure fast and easy reading and effortless understanding.

There is, indeed, a secret that will guarantee that anyone who knows it, and who uses it, according to the rules laid down will have not only a zestful life, but also an inner peace and an outer glow of personality that will make it possible for him to attract and influence others in a way that is deeply satisfying and utterly fulfilling.

The written word—this book, for example—is enough to unveil this secret. It's good to have friendly contacts with other humans, but this secret can be found, and used, without any other help. I know this, because that's the way I found it. I was a Buddhist in my youth—a convinced and practicing Buddhist. I was tormented by the awful fears that come with the Buddhist belief in reincarnation. The Buddhists say we are all headed for punishment in the afterlife for our misdeeds in this life. The punishment, they think, will come with reincarnation, by being brought back to life on this earth in some lower, less happy form, possibly as an insect, or one of the lower animals.

I escaped from the torment of that ghastly doctrine at the age of seventeen when I picked up a plainly-written book which told the secret that we will describe later. I took the words of the man who wrote that book into my heart, and have lived by them ever since. And in all modesty I can witness that my life has been happy and satisfying beyond my wildest dreams since that day when I learned the secret. Now I want to pass it on, to all who will read about it. There's no need to pay a lot of money to an Oriental guru. The secret is free. It's up to you to use it in the way it was meant to be used. If you do this, you are about to experience some wonderful surprises.

Eddy Ie Swieson
Washington, D.C.
April, 1978

Good News About Trouble

1

The Truth about Trouble

I think this is a good time, right here at the beginning, to tell you some of the things I have learned about people and their troubles.

Trouble, and the people involved in it, have been my full-time concern for about a quarter of a century. And my unwavering aim has been to lead them to an understanding and acceptance of the great transforming secret that insures a zestful, happy, productive life. Along the way, I have acquired a liberal education in human nature.

My nearly twenty-five years of counseling have convinced me that most people are too close to their problems, too deeply and emotionally involved in them, to find the way out by themselves.

When trouble closes in on a man or woman, it puts its victim in a sort of mental and spiritual maze from which, to the victim, there seems to be no exit. Like hysterical victims trapped by a fire, their emotions become their worst enemy. It takes a friend, viewing their plight with detachment and concern and with clear vision, to point the way.

So my first word of advice to anyone in trouble—any kind of trouble—is: "Don't hesitate to ask for help."

I have also learned that the following are universally acceptable truths:

The odds are about 100 to 1 that you are not as bad as you think you are. No situation is as bad, or as good, as it seems to those who are closest to it. It is characteristic of human nature to overdramatize both problems and pleasures.

The human conscience also tends to exaggerate. That's the way it gets attention.

But if your problem is ego, instead of a troubled conscience, you're a more difficult case, but not hopeless. Ego trouble sneaks up on you quietly. You've probably lost a lot of friends already, and if you still have some left you are going to lose them, too. Eventually you will find yourself virtually alone and miserable. Nobody can be zestful, successful and happy all by himself. The danger signal to watch for: the growing list of "friends" you never see any more.

Boredom is at the root of much of this world's trouble. The danger line has been crossed when the routines of life—getting and spending, eating and drinking, working and sleeping—begin to "get you down." When that happens, your defenses are "down," too. You are at that moment vulnerable to the temptation to try some artificial kind of excitement—drugs, drink, sexual pleasures and the like. If you read the newspapers you know what can happen next.

Boredom is a complex emotion. Basically, it is the result of a lack of vision; the inability to see the exciting challenges in everyday life. You may prefer to call it the lack of imagination, or the absence of a creative urge. One ancient man of wisdom discovered the "vision" link between boredom and trouble some thousands of years before Eddy Swieson was born, so I can't claim the discovery. I merely point it out. This early thinker wrote: "Where there is no vision, the people perish." What he was saying in modern words was, "Be sure your eyes do not deceive you. . . . Be sure you really *see* what you are looking at."

The proper interpretation of trouble can be tricky, even to one whose adult life has been spent answering calls for help.

Not long ago an intelligent, ambitious young man, one who was well liked and admired by his friends, came to me with a strange and unexpected story. He was obviously upset and deeply depressed, and this was what he told me:

"My boss is 'mad' at me and I can't figure out

why! I think he has it in mind to fire me, and I don't want to lose that job. It's intensely interesting, there's a wide-open door to advancement and I think I'm doing a better-than-good job. He doesn't find fault with what I'm doing, he just doesn't seem to like me any more. He's always angry with me. I've got to find out what is the matter. How can I do it?"

I questioned him, and listened at length to what he would tell me about his employer and about the business and how it was doing. It seemed that sales were declining, and that the employer was facing payments on loans that for the time being, at least, could not be covered by profits, and would have to be refinanced.

Though I have never been a businessman I became convinced the trouble was rooted in human nature—the employer's human nature. So I told the young man I thought the boss was "mad" at himself over a business miscalculation and was simply unloading his ire on this employee. I believed the young man had no reason to fear.

I suggested to him that instead of a career crisis, he was facing a rare opportunity to be helpful to another human being in trouble. And I urged him to forget the angry words and try to find ways to help his troubled boss.

There was doubt on the young man's face as he departed, but he said he would try my suggestion.

Weeks later we met on the street, and the young man didn't even mention the trouble. And as he turned to go, I remarked that I hoped things were going well with him.

"Oh, yes," he said. "I almost forgot to thank you. You were right. I asked him what I could do to help him, and the boss thanked me with tears in his eyes. Everything's great."

The moral of this story is: Don't hesitate to ask for help, or to give help. Pride can cause you needless pain. It can destroy you.

Fear and inexperience are another pair of troublemakers. I learned this by painful personal experience.

Early in life I was handed a job that I had dreamed about but never really hoped for. My supervisor, a man of good heart and sympathetic understanding, believed in delegating authority to his staff. He expected them to be "self-starters." But for many months in this dream job I was handicapped by fear of doing the wrong thing. So I worried and waited for orders which did not come. I did only the routine things. Though I pondered taking action on my own, I held back because I didn't want to make a bad mistake and lose this wonderful job. The worry brought on both physical and mental fatigue. I was exhausted every evening, even though I had not really worked hard. On top of all this tiring worry, I found I was getting bored with this "wonderful" job, mainly because I was not doing what was expected, because of my fear of making mistakes.

Finally I could take no more, so I went privately to a fellow staff member for advice. He gave it, quickly and briefly: "Eddy," he said, "you're supposed to be a general, not a private. You've got to run the war in your sector."

So I gritted my teeth and began to run my own war, and a whole new world opened to me. Though I did make mistakes, I was much more often right. There was a new excitement in the work. The boredom and worry that had polluted my mind and spirit disappeared. I could hardly wait to get to the office in the morning to face some new challenge. And, to my secret delight, the "boss" made it clear that the "new Eddy" was the one he thought he had hired in the first place.

In this great country the makings of a richer, fuller life are all around us, always within reach for those with vision clear enough to see them.

If any overall, general statement can be made about the generation living here today it is that too many of us are too close to the trees to see the grandeur and beauty of the forest. Too many of us are too concerned with the small problems to recognize the really big one: the problem of living our relatively short span of life in the meaningful, zestful way the Creator intended.

Now don't get me wrong. I'm not arguing

that you need to have your head, or your eyes examined if you are one of those who are depressed or desperately unhappy.

Indeed, I agree that this world is a pretty bad neighborhood to have to spend our lives in. It's certainly not the kind of place any of us would want to live in forever. And it's probably going to get worse as it becomes more crowded.

So, if you are depressed and pessimistic about your own outlook you may have good reasons. But there is a way—a tried and proven way—to rise above the things that depress you and poison your mind and spirit.

It is contained in a secret formula designed to guarantee a happy, useful, productive life to any and all who will embrace it and live by it. It offers a transforming power that has kept civilization alive in this world for the last two thousand years. And one of the strangest things about it is that it works *best* when everything else in life is at its *worst*; and it is most readily available to those most desperately in need of it. More about this later.

You've heard about the fabled wisdom of Solomon, the ancient King of Israel who was supposed to have been the wisest man who ever lived. All indications are that Solomon died an unhappy man. It may have been because nobody was wiser than Solomon in his day, so there was nobody on earth for him to turn to for advice. Besides, by the time he died,

Solomon didn't have many friends left. So he would have had difficulty finding a source of friendly advice in any case.

Millions of people today are, in many ways, wiser than Solomon, and vastly more fortunate. In spite of all the wealth the ancient king amassed, Solomon died bemoaning his belief that everything man does on this earth is useless and senseless. Now we have knowledge, and proof, that contradicts this.

Now we know when a person reaches his absolute physical and spiritual bottom, when he dangles from the end of his rope, when he can endure no more and wishes for death; we know now that even at that low point he is only an instant away from a life-changing transformation—if he wants it, and asks for it.

We know, too, that Solomon, even if he had lived today, would have got himself into trouble. He broke all the rules and got his priorities twisted and reversed.

His great wealth came from crushing competition and the extorting of heavy taxes from merchants traveling through his domain.

He monopolized the infant iron industry, and turned it to production of weapons for his vast armies and his fortresses. Much of his wealth was poured into the military coffers.

He ruled by force and oppression and exploitation. He created diplomatic alliances by marrying princesses and other royal women of the surrounding kingdoms, and ended with

700 wives and 300 concubines.

His writings show that he knew, near the end, that he had trampled the human rights of everyone whose life he touched, including his wives.

In this enlightened day we know that when a road is paved with the bodies of people exploited or cheated or ignored in their time of need, it cannot lead to success and happiness. It took Solomon a lifetime to find this out.

In his last days, King Solomon was haunted by fear that any angry Creator was going to judge him harshly for his evil ways. He expected life after death, but he died with fear in his heart that it would not be a very happy life for him, after his monstrous life of self-indulgence here on earth.

Like Solomon, the troubled, unhappy people of today have got their priorities twisted or reversed. But for the troubled people of today there is hope that Solomon knew nothing about.

In his fabled wisdom, Solomon maintained that the world would never change; that every generation would go on making the same mistakes as the last, that to try for permanent improvement of the human condition was "useless" and "vanity."

He may have been right about the *world*.

But we know, now, that individuals who live in this world CAN be changed.

That is what this book is about.

In the following chapters I propose to introduce you to the secret of inner change, inner peace and freedom from fear.

In a single moment, your life in this shoddy world can be transformed into an exciting time of accomplishment and pleasure.

I urge you to read about this secret, to embrace it, and to live by it.

If you do, I'm sure you'll like it.

But, if you try it and don't like it, you lose nothing. The return of your misery and troubles is guaranteed.

2

Where Did I Go Wrong?

Now let's get down to the nitty-gritty.

If you are in trouble, any kind of trouble, you're in the same boat with a lot of others. You are not unique. People who are troubled and distressed are inclined to think nobody else ever had it so bad. But I can assure you of this: after twenty-five years as a sympathetic listener and adviser I have learned that troubles of all kinds follow the same general pattern, with only minor variations. People in trouble all ask about the same anxious questions. "Where—or how—did I go wrong?" and "What can I do to make amends?"

Now I'm not belittling anybody's trouble, for I have wept and prayed with so many tortured people that I know how real and tragic the troubles of this world can be.

The reason why all kinds of trouble follow the same general pattern is because they all have the same roots. It is important to understand that every kind of trouble that plagues human beings on this earth originates in exactly the same way:

Trouble starts when someone breaks one of the laws of nature.

Some prefer to call them God's laws. But whatever name you choose, the laws of nature, or of God, are the age-old code that has kept the human race on a more or less even keel since the beginning of time.

They are precise and immutable. Ignorance of them is no excuse. If you ignore them, or violate them, you pay a price.

In theological terms, breaking the laws of nature—God's laws—is called "sin." But let's leave the theological language to the theologians. Just remember, the next time you are entangled in trouble of some kind, the origin is a violation of one of the laws of nature, either by something you have done or said, or a violation by another person.

Take the case of a drunk driver as a simple example. If he hits your car and damages it and possibly injures you or someone else riding with you, he is the source of your trouble; he has violated one of the laws of nature by getting drunk. And if the drunk driver happens to be you, the penalty is immeasurably greater. On top of whatever price man's law may exact, you may be tortured for months or years with intense remorse and self-condemnation.

Suicide is another violation of the laws of

nature that spreads trouble far afield from the desperate victim himself. Family, friends and the community suffer, too, even more than the person who committed this crime against nature.

Now some reader is about to say he hasn't the vaguest idea of what the laws of nature require of him, so how can he avoid breaking some of them?

That's a simple question, and here's the simple answer:

All of us, fortunately, have a built-in legal reference library called "conscience" that spots a potential violation of the laws of nature the moment it enters the mind.

If every member of the human race had been put together without a conscience, the laws of nature long ago would have been superseded by the law of the jungle, and civilization wouldn't be even a dim memory.

"Let your conscience be your guide," may sound trite to the sophisticated, but it is a basic truth, and one of the cornerstones of the successful life.

The existence of conscience is a major factor in modern law enforcement. The experts in crime detection know that anyone who lies is going to get a jolt from his conscience—a faster heartbeat or an upward spurt of blood pressure, or a cold sweat. From this knowledge it was just one easy step to the invention of the lie detector.

If you'd like to test yourself to find out if something you may be thinking of, or planning, is a violation of the laws of nature, there is a foolproof way to do it. I call it the "repellent test." It's simple to use, and I can't imagine how it could possibly give the wrong answer. It works like this:

Run down the following check list before you make a decision:

1. Will it cause physical harm to me or anyone else?

2. Is it going to make someone angry, unhappy, resentful?

3. Is it going to needlessly complicate my life, or some other person's life?

4. What would I say if someone else were going to do this thing and came to me for advice?

5. Do I have to lie or cheat or be evasive to accomplish this thing?

6. If I go ahead and do it, is my conscience going to worry me into insomnia?

7. Does it involve breaking the laws of the city, state or nation?

8. If my mother or father or friends knew I was doing this, what would they think of me?

9. If there is a risk involved, is the end result worth it?

Check with your conscience after each question. If there is any repellent reaction, you are heading for trouble, and you had better drop the whole idea.

There's a simpler test if you are in such a hurry that you haven't time for all this.

If the plan is going to cost you the loss of friendships, or if there is any chance at all that you may be ostracized or isolated from your friends if you go ahead with it—then *don't*.

To lose even one friend takes a measure of joy out of your life.

To lose a whole group of friends is disastrous.

Nobody can possibly be happy and successful in a social vacuum. Remember what they say about the tango: it takes at least two to do it. The same rule holds for happy, zestful living. Two is the minimum. The more, the happier.

On the other hand, anybody can be *unhappy* all by himself, *especially* all by himself.

Man was created to be a social being. That's the reason why he has created so many towns and cities to live in; these are places where he can join his strength and his talents with the strength and talents of others living nearby and thereby speed the advance of civilization and enhance the well-being of all mankind.

Now if all this sounds silly and frivolous to you, please reread the last couple of pages and really think about them. To ignore the warnings of conscience is the equivalent of asking for trouble. And be warned: There is no way to escape punishment if you deliberately violate the laws of nature and of God.

Now let's be a bit more specific about these age-old laws that separate man from the animals and hold civilization together.

What specific acts will turn you into a lawbreaker and bring certain retribution?

Some are so obvious they hardly need listing, but just in case your conscience may be somewhat less sensitive than it should be, we'll start with the most obvious:

I think almost any conscience would revolt at murder. But you are also beyond the bounds if your conduct is drunken and disorderly, if you commit physical violence, if you are habitually angry, jealous, covetous and sexually immoral.

Many modern humans seem to be equipped with the kind of conscience that accepts gossip as an activity, without too much protest. Or possibly they are just ignoring its protests because gossip has become so accepted by modern society that there are special sections devoted to it in the newspapers. But gossip can bring misery to other human beings. And if that happens, the purveyor of the gossip is breaking God's law. Even the truth, if the telling of it brings harm, is outlawed by nature.

Then there is stealing—both outright theft and theft by deception—greed, deceit, indecency, slander, excessive pride, carelessness, thoughtlessness, and so on and on.

The police may never be involved in most of

the crimes just mentioned, but having to hide your crime from family, friends and associates, and the constant fear that they may learn your secret, or at least suspect it, is punishment worse, in some ways, than a prison term.

And now we come to one of the worst and most persistent violators of the laws of nature: the untamed human tongue!

The tongue commits more crimes and touches off more violence than all the rest of the body combined. The course of history has been changed for the worse, governments have been toppled, bloody wars have been started, revolutions have been incited and millions have been slaughtered senselessly by nothing more than a tongue guided by an evil mind and aided by a talent for oratory.

The most repulsive example of what the tongue can do, in recent history, is the brief, blood-spattered history of Hitler's Germany. The whole tragedy of World War II was touched off by the persistent and oratorical repetition of a lie so big and so impossible that when lightning did not strike the orator for repeating it over and over, millions of Germans began to accept it as truth. And they followed Hitler to destruction.

For most of us the wayward tongue does nothing so dramatic, but it is causing divorce, breaking friendships, and driving children away from home by the hundreds of thousands.

Even the verbal trapping of a victim in a practical joke can turn into a major crime, as in one incident I witnessed myself.

It happened at a lavish banquet, a joyful affair with much laughter and happy conversation. Two men sat across the table from each other. They were nominal friends, close enough to know each other's habits. One was a practical joker, the other was so fond of food that eating was an obsession with him, a fact well known to the joker.

The soup course came, and it was boiling hot. Our practical joker pretended to take a large spoonful, and then remarked in a loud voice to his friend across the table: "This is the most wonderful soup I have ever tasted. Try a spoonful quickly while it is still warm!"

The glutton eagerly filled a soupspoon and put it in his mouth. Unable to spit it out at the banquet table, he gave a muffled cry and swallowed the boiling mixture, badly burning his mouth, throat and stomach. Moments later he collapsed. He died on the way to the hospital.

If it's your tongue that's causing your trouble, you have only one simple remedy to remember: an angry word or an evil thought is harmless to others until it is spoken. So pause and think before you say it. The damage is irretrievable afterward.

Angry words, false accusations, foolish curses—for the normal human being these are among the most difficult sins to forgive and forget.

The memory of an angry outburst lives on and on. The scars may never go away.

When an untamed tongue explodes with anger it frequently goads the person who is its target into the same kind of violation of nature's law. So, if you feel you simply must blow off steam, the best place is in the privacy of your bedroom. Lock the door, walk over to the mirror and watch the angry face that stares back at you as you loose your verbal blast. The sight should frighten you into a more reasonable state of mind.

The foregoing are just a few among many hundreds of suggestions that could have been cited, to help you discover for yourself the answer to the question: "Where did I go wrong?"

If you think you have found the answer, you're moving in the right direction. But before you can move very far you will come up against some more puzzling questions: "Now that I know how I got into this mess, what can I do about it? How can I get out of it?"

I will tell you how others have found highly successful answers to these questions in the course of the next few chapters.

3

Detours to Avoid

Up to this point I have tried to make two things clear: (1) that every kind of trouble starts in the same way; it starts when somebody breaks one of God's laws, and (2) that if you know exactly what got you into trouble, and acknowledge it, you have taken an important first step toward getting out of it.

The importance of being exact and precise in the description of your trouble, when you are talking to one who is trying to help you, cannot be overemphasized. The late Adlai Stevenson used to tell a story that makes this very point.

He told of a telephone operator in a large hotel who began to get a series of calls, starting at about midnight. They all came from a man who obviously had been drinking too much. Every half hour or so he would call again with the same question: "When is the bar going to open?" And every time he called he seemed to be in worse condition than before.

Finally, in exasperation, the operator snapped: "Look here, sir. I've told you six times that the bar opens at 11 a.m. And I might as well warn you that when they see the condition you have got yourself into, they won't let you in!"

There was a second or two of silence on the other end of the line. Then the inebriated voice came through in tones of righteous indignation. "In? In? Did I say I wanted in? I been in all night! I want *OUT*!"

If our inebriated friend had made that clear statement of his problem several hours earlier it would have saved him a terrible hangover and the operator a lot of irritation.

So let's presume you have reached the point of full surrender. For once in your life—maybe for the first time—you have a problem that has no solution; you are completely baffled. You can't imagine how you, a person of normal intelligence, could have reached such a point, when everything seemed to be going so smoothly so recently. You have finally admitted to yourself that your life is unmanageable, and that you've got to have help.

This is a crucial moment.

You can get into worse trouble if you put your trust in the wrong kind of counselor.

Avoid pill-pushers, medical quacks, Oriental gurus—in short avoid all who offer to sell you a shortcut to peace of mind for a bargain price.

These are detours; a waste of time and money.

Look for a trusted friend—one whose life appears to be untroubled, one who shows the outward glow of inner happiness. Ask him where to go for advice and counsel.

Or, if you have no friends left, if you have lost them all, then get in touch with me. I can find you the kind of friend you need. Time is important when you reach the point of humbling yourself and admitting to another human being that you are helpless.

You are ready to listen and to do what it takes to escape the misery that has trapped you.

The evening paper in Washington, D.C., where I live, recently carried the tragic story of a wealthy local resident, a man active in the social and business world, the father of three healthy children and the husband of a loyal and loving wife. His business was booming and there was no outward sign of inner trouble. Yet, when his wife and children returned from an evening at the theater they found him lying on the floor in a puddle of blood, a bullet hole in his head, a suicide note in one hand, a revolver in the other.

The newspaper reported that his friends could think of no reason why he should have taken his life. "He had everything to live for," they told the reporters. "Why did he do it?"

The only clue came from his wife, who said that he was "not a religious man" but that he had suddenly, in recent weeks, started going to church—alone—and that his checkbook showed he had been giving large contributions to the church.

That turned on a signal light in my mind. I've seen this happen before. It's one of the ways a desperate man signals for help.

There is a strange notion, that apparently has been around for centuries, that the way to get yourself out of a personal mess is to do some big favor for God. Like going to church every Sunday until things begin to look better, or saying some ritual prayer over and over to prove you really mean it.

Now you'd think it would be plain to an intelligent twentieth-century person that sitting in a church pew, singing a few hymns, putting a large check in the collection plate and shaking hands with the preacher on the way out, are not going to make much of an impression on the almighty Creator of the universe.

But people in trouble don't worry about logic. I feel that the man who committed suicide was signaling for help by going to church. And I fear that when he found it a useless detour that did not help him find the road to recovery, it was too much for his desperate spirit to bear.

How much more sense it would have made for him to seek out the pastor or a counselor on a weekday. If he had done this he might be alive today, and his family and friends would have been spared much suffering.

Attending and supporting a church is good spiritual exercise, but if you do it only to get into the good graces of God, it's a waste of time.

If you have broken a law of nature, one of God's laws, you can't buy or bribe your way out of your trouble.

There's an old-fashioned word that applies, and we might as well start using it right here. When you violate one of the laws of nature—God's laws—the theologians call it "sin."

Now "sin" is a disease of the spirit. Like other diseases, it spreads as it develops. Once it has got a start it gradually spreads a poison through the spiritual being. Then it begins to infect and pollute the mind and distort the thinking processes. And in the final stages, the disease of "sin" can make a person physically sick.

At this level, the sufferer from sin-sickness may go to a doctor, where he is most likely to be told his illness is psychosomatic—it's all in his mind.

I think there could be a giant step forward in the health sciences if the medical schools of the country required their students to take basic studies in the spiritual make-up of their future patients. For, after all, medical science readily acknowledges that a human being is a complicated combination of physical, mental and spiritual elements. And when any one of the three parts gets out of order, the whole man suffers.

I dream of the day when the medical profession will give practical, professional recognition to the spiritual element. When a doctor finds that he has a patient with a spiritual illness, it should be common practice to refer him to a specialist in spiritual matters.

To tell him, instead, that his suffering is "psychosomatic" amounts, in my view, to malpractice.

"Sin" and the spiritual poisoning and pollution it generates, are not something new that the preachers have cooked up just to boost their business. As a disease, "sin" can be diagnosed as accurately as any other disease. And its progress from the earliest signs of infection can be predicted as accurately as the spread of any physical ailment.

For example, the earliest sign of spiritual poisoning caused by sin is a tendency toward moral confusion. The sufferer, in the early stages, often brushes aside the warnings of his conscience as false and exaggerated. He sees no harm in a few small departures from honesty and morality.

Next, he becomes more outspoken in defense of his questionable new views of right and wrong. He sometimes wanders off into slanderous and foolish talk. His pride is easily injured when others disagree with views which even he, deep inside, knows are wrong.

His personal relationships become strained. Friendships don't last long, and are frequently broken off in anger.

As the sufferer from the disease of "sin" becomes more isolated he develops resentments against his lost friends. He draws farther and farther inside himself. He is beset by a smouldering anger that flares into flame at the slightest excuse.

As the critical stage approaches, the disease of "sin" causes the loss of enthusiasm for the good and constructive things of life. The sufferer begins to seek out companions who share his perverted views.

In the final stages, the sufferer from sin may be tortured by fear. In a fleeting moment of introspection he may realize, for the first time, the depths to which he has sunk. He still knows what is right and what is wrong, but he no longer has a choice between good and evil. His life truly has been taken out of his control.

Soon after my arrival in this country from Indonesia I met a man who became one of my dearest friends. His story is a classic example of what the disease of sin can do.

As a youth he loved to sail, and he loved the sea. So he decided on a sudden impulse, to become a sailor, and he traveled over the world and visited many countries.

Outgoing and impetuous as he was, he eagerly sampled every new pleasure and adventure he came across: wine, women gambling, extortion and all manner of evil perversions. His decline was rapid. Within a couple of years, he made his way back to this country sick in body, mind and spirit, unemployable and homeless.

Anxious relatives finally traced him to skid row in a large eastern city, took him to a shelter and spent thousands of dollars trying to cure his diseases and "straighten him out" mentally and spiritually. Nothing seemed to work.

He told me that during that time he kept a revolver hidden nearby, and frequently decided to use it on himself, but was stopped by something inside him at the last minute.

As he lay one day, groaning and hopeless, he took out of his pocket a pamphlet that someone had given him. Through hazy, reddened eyes he painfully read it, and way down inside this bit of human wreckage he felt his conscience frantically signaling, "This is it! This is it! You can live again!"

The pamphlet pointed out to him that his troubles all had been caused by his habitual breaking of the laws of God and nature.

And then it revealed the Great Truth I mentioned earlier in this book: There is a way to have your life transformed instantaneously.

"All you have to do is recognize that the God of all creation is ready and eager to do it for you, and then humble yourself and ask Him to do it!" the pamphlet said.

You don't have to do a lot of good deeds to prove you are sincere.

You don't have to take a course of study to learn how to get this life-changing experience.

You don't have to seek out any monk or hermit to learn a secret routine or ritual.

There's no need for a shape-up period. It's done "while you wait."

Then my friend read this final passage:

"The God who created you knows your weakness and your needs. He knows you are sincere. He who created you, and everything else that exists, will have no difficulty reshaping your thoughts, feelings, will and actions. He can do it this minute!"

My friend said he shook his head to clear his thoughts and find the "catch" in this proposition. "That would have to be a miracle," he said to himself. "And why not?" a voice seemed to answer. "For God, miracles are 'business as usual.' It's His efficient way of doing things."

My friend began to weep. And it was then that it happened! Just as the pamphlet promised!

It was this same man—many years after the day of his spiritual transformation—who took me by the hand when I arrived in America, an awed and frightened Chinese immigrant. It was this man, miraculously transformed in an instant by God, who helped to mold my mental and spiritual outlook in the fifteen years I have lived and worked here.

Now that I have reluctantly introduced a theological word—"sin"—to this nontheological discussion, I'd better hasten to define it.

Sin is any willful deviation from what conscience and the laws of God and nature require of you.

It is vanity, selfishness, perversion, dishonesty, unfaithfulness, rebellion against higher authority, defiance of the law (man's law), the breaking of solemn promises and agreements. In short, it is willful distortion of the natural order of things in any way.

You really can't help recognizing sin. Every human being who reaches maturity instinctively knows sin the minute he sees it, hears it, or even thinks about it. Every one of us is equipped with an inner warning mechanism that sets off an alarm when we even ponder the violation of one of the God-given laws of nature and civilization.

It's when we ignore these warnings that we get into trouble.

If you, perchance, are one who knows he is guilty of any of these willful distortions, you already know the bad news: Habitual sin can kill you, just as surely as cancer.

But now, the good news: Sin doesn't have to kill you.

If you have had enough unhappiness and misery. If you have had enough of the punishment that you brought on yourself. If you sincerely want to return to the company of successful, happy, friendly, law-abiding people. If you want to get back in tune with creation and the Creator, just say so. The job can be done while you wait. He is ready when you are.

4

What Will God Think?

It's tough to have to admit you have been trying to prove you are smarter than God.

It's even tougher to confess you have made a mess of it.

So it's only natural to feel fearful and utterly miserable when you first try to make contact with the all-wise, all-knowing Spirit of the universe himself. If you felt any other way you could hardly fool Him into thinking you were sincere.

It may help to remember you are not alone. At this very moment thousands of others across the world are sure to be facing this same spiritual crisis. And in the decades and centuries of the past many millions of others have traveled the same tear-stained road. I, myself, am one of them.

When I reached this point in my search for God, I fully expected to be struck down by lightning, or something worse, as punishment for the sins I confessed. It was not until afterward that it occurred to me God knew in advance everything I had so painfully detailed to Him, and that if He had wanted to strike me down He would have done it long before He heard my confession.

But I'm sure it is for the best that we all come to this crisis in our lives fully expecting the worst kind of punishment. For, after all, most of us have to acknowledge spiritual crimes that deserve it.

Besides, if we came before the Almighty thinking that all we had to do was say "I'm sorry" it would be a waste of time.

I still remember a day, when I was very young and my parents were out of the house temporarily, and I decided to ignore a stern parental order to stay out of the cabinet where they kept the most expensive chinaware.

I climbed up the kitchen stool-ladder and reached for one of the most delicate pieces, one I had always admired for its bright colors. I clutched it carefully to my body as I started down the ladder. But as a novice at ladder-climbing I missed one rung. And in a sudden panic I dropped the precious chinaware to save myself, and it crashed and broke into a thousand pieces.

Almost before the enormity of what had happened came to me, I heard the front door opening, and the voices of my parents filtered through. What should I do? Run and hide?

Leave home and never return? Tell them the cat did it?

But there was no time to ponder alternatives. My father, at that moment, walked through the door. And in a glance I saw on his face that look of anger and irritation mixed with deep affection. So I just stood there in the middle of the floor and wept bitter tears in a voice the neighbors could hear many houses away. All who heard it could make no mistake about it. My wails of sorrow amounted to a sincere confession of guilt. I expected the kind of thrashing that I knew I deserved.

But my father took me by the hand and led me into my bedroom. There he explained to me that what I had destroyed could never be replaced, and the precious set of dishes and cups would never again be complete.

"Every time you see this china set, and the empty space for the missing piece," he said, "all the rest of your life you will remember what happens when a boy disobeys his parents."

He spoke the truth. I still remember. No thrashing that he could have administered would have had a more lasting impression. Even today, in middle age, the twinges of guilt remain when I think of that incident.

God works the same way. A troubled conscience is punishment that is both severe and effective, and also long-lasting.

I can see, now, that the outcome of this little incident would have been harder on me, and less effective, if I had tried to "blame it on the cat" or had run away.

So, when you think you are ready for your first conference with God, examine your thoughts and your innermost feelings.

If, in your heart, you still think someone else "made you" break one of God's laws, and that you are not entirely to blame, then postpone the showdown. You are not ready.

Don't try to argue with God.

Above all, don't lie to God. That is the ultimate folly. If you are not going to be open and honest about everything in your life, it is better not to talk to Him at all.

But let's presume that—since you are reading this book—you are, indeed, tired of living the life of a fugitive from God's law. If you now recognize yourself as the prodigal son in Christ's parable, and you honestly feel you don't deserve more than what the prodigal son asked for—the scraps from the table that were thrown to the pigs—then the time is ripe, the moment has arrived.

You are ready to experience a personal contact with almighty God.

Take careful note of everything that is happening, because you will remember this day for the rest of your life.

If you are really sincere and fully humbled, you are about to experience the mystery of a life-changing transformation.

You will know, without any doubt

whatsoever, that God himself has reached down and touched you.

Your eyes will be opened. Everything you have been seeing all your life will suddenly look fresh and different in a happy, unexplainable way.

You will feel the kind of joy, or even greater joy, that might come if you had unexpectedly won a million-dollar lottery.

You will have an overwhelming urge to tell somebody, anybody, everybody about the wonderful thing that has happened.

Your heart will feel like it's bursting with love.

You will wonder how you could have been so blind for so long.

You will understand, clearly, at last, that God never wanted to punish you for the sins you committed. He wanted you only to stop sinning.

He wanted only to cure you of the disease of sin that had so poisoned your body, mind and spirit that you had lost control of your own life.

When your eyes are opened by the divine Spirit you will see that you were acting as if under orders from an evil source.

You will understand, then, that the *real you* did not want to do what you were doing; that you did these things because a spiritual poisoning had distorted your vision, muffled the voice of conscience and weakened your will.

In other words, you'll find out that you have

been *spiritually sick*. You will know that you have been restored to *spiritual health*.

The wonder of this miraculous thing is that the transformation is instantaneous!

That's the way God practices His spiritual medicine.

Now you have the right to ask: "How do you know all this? Can you prove it?"

I'll take the first question first.

I know what I have told you is true because I have told you exactly what happened to me. And I am sure God didn't pick me out for any special favors. I have heard many others describe their own experience in the same terms.

How can I prove it?

If your eyes and ears are operating normally, you shouldn't need proof from me. Watch the lives of people around you. Or read the newspapers. I can quote some very prominent witnesses.

Some of the most notorious individuals of this century have been transformed before your eyes, and the miracle of it has been published and broadcast in detail all over the world.

Consider the architect of the scandals of Watergate, Charles "Chuck" Colson. This former scoundrel, a mastermind of the political trickery and illegalities that toppled the Nixon administration, has done a 180-degree about-face.

While serving a prison term that he readily admits he deserved, Colson was introduced to the secret of inner transformation by a friend, and he grasped it eagerly, and began to live by it. He tells the story in his book, *Born Again*.

In prison he was appalled by the tragic waste of hundreds of thousands of lives behind the prison walls. Now a free man, Colson has rededicated his life to a fast-growing, nationwide movement that is reaching into the prisons.

The transformation of this one man—Charles Colson—has brought new hope and new meaning to the lives of thousands who still live behind bars.

This all grew out of one heart-to-heart talk with God, by one man—a man whose personal disgrace and criminal conviction brought him face-to-face with the more important truth: that he was breaking the laws of God.

Or consider that former revolutionary, that ex-enemy of the American way of life and everything it stands for: Eldridge Cleaver.

A leader of the militant and violent Black Panthers, Cleaver was an outlaw and a fugitive from justice. He fled from country to country, seeking support for his revolutionary views, but finding only disappointment in those countries supposedly sympathetic to him.

Crushed by his failures and in a mood of deep depression and desperation—at the very lowest point of his life—Cleaver learned of the secret that could transform him.

Like Colson, he recognized it at once as the answer to his unspoken prayers. This was what he really had been searching for even in his revolutionary days. So, like his old political enemy, Colson, he embraced this newly revealed truth and began to live by it.

He came back to the United States to face the punishment he deserved under man's law. But the new joy in his heart would not be silenced. He traveled over the country telling of his new life and the new Eldridge Cleaver, and the pure joy of knowing he was now living in accordance with God's laws.

Thousands of new friends have rallied to help him. Some of his former revolutionary colleagues have abandoned their violent ways and joined him.

But the wonder of wonders is to see and hear Colson and Cleaver side by side on a public platform, singing the same happy songs, and embracing each other as brothers under the code of laws laid down by the Creator of us all.

The stories they tell differ widely until near the end. Then they join in solid confirmation of the great truth that when a man reaches the depths of adversity and misery, he is only one step away from a new life, zestful and fulfilling, if he submits to the transforming power of God.

You may never get a chance to meet either one of these gentlemen. But look around you.

There are thousands of others just like them. They don't get the publicity, but they DO have the POWER. They can whisper the secret and show you the way to this exciting new life, just as effectively as their better-known brothers. What's more, they are eager to do it.

Watch the lives of people around you. Single out a few who seem to be in a miserable mess. Keep an eye on these, especially. Sooner or later one of them suddenly will show all the signs of transformation into a happy, successful human being.

Get acquainted with this person. Tell him what you have seen, and ask him what happened. The chances are he will be one who can pass the secret on to you. It won't take long to find out.

Now if you don't have the time to wait and watch, if you are already so deeply troubled that you want to escape from it right now, then get in touch with me, in person, or by phone or by mail. The publisher of this book will know where to find me, if you can't. I'll find a friend for you, or help you myself.

One of the ironies of the latter half of the twentieth century is the fascination of so many of our dissatisfied youth with the Oriental mystics.

Here in the West we live in a civilization that has raised the spiritual level of the whole world. Yet our press, many of our best-selling books and even television personalities are beating the drums to advertise the wonders of such man-made religions as Transcendental Meditation, Yoga and the like.

What a waste of time and energy! What a useless detour for troubled minds and spirits!

Yet, many reputable people testify with enthusiasm to the relief they have received from the stresses and strains of everyday living, and from fatigue and anxiety as a result of these mystic formulas.

I have heard or read of such testimonials from members of Congress, astronauts, Pentagon generals, Wall Street tycoons, Broadway playwrights, scientists, businessmen, doctors, housewives and students.

The amount of money they spend and the lengthy courses of study they endure to acquire this inner peace and spiritual relaxation seems to prove at least one useful point. It proves that the world is full of people with a deep spiritual hunger. And it redoubles my determination to tell them all how to get what they are seeking the easy way—and without cost.

But there seems to be a peculiar tendency, particularly among Americans, to suspect that there's a catch when anything is offered "free of charge." The idea seems to be that "if it's free, you get exactly what you pay for—nothing."

In the world of material things this probably is true. But in the spiritual realm, money doesn't count. It may, in fact, be a barrier.

For God, it is enough if you obey His laws, join His circle of friends and consult Him regularly in privacy. He can suggest other ways for you to spend your money.

5

Is God Really There?

Yes!

But maybe you'd rather hear another expert speak on this subject. I have some very good first-hand evidence myself, but a man in my occupation *has* to have it, or he would be living a lie.

So let's hear, instead, from a scientist, one of the greatest of our generation: the late Dr. Wernher von Braun, the designer of our great rockets and the leader of our race to the moon, and beyond.

Here are some of the things Dr. Von Braun said in a lecture at Belmont Abbey College, Belmont, North Carolina, in 1972:

"One cannot be exposed to the order and beauty of the universe without conceding there must be a divine intent behind it."

A listener questioned him directly: "Is there really a God?"

Von Braun replied, "Must we light a candle

to see the sun?

"The more we understand the universe and the intricacies of its operation, the more sense we have to marvel at its Creator.

"Science and religion are not incompatible. While science tries to learn more about creation, religion tries to learn more about the Creator."

It was that pioneer of celestial navigation, the ancient astronomer Galileo, who put the same thought into words for the first time. Persecuted for his theory that the earth revolves around the sun, and accused of heresy by the Inquisition, he boldly replied to a hostile questioner: "Religion is meant to tell us how to go to heaven; it is the role of science to tell us how the heavens go."

Belatedly, his views are coming into their own among the leaders of both religion and science. Even some of those who have decried the teaching of the Bible story of creation in the schools in the past have abandoned their efforts to keep it out.

Now, only a few years after that declaration of faith by Dr. Von Braun, Michigan State University, Iowa State University, and other major schools are offering courses on the "theory" that God created the world and all that's in it. New textbooks are being prepared, based on the book of Genesis, and other schools are falling in line.

"It's the hottest thing going on in science

today," says Professor John Moore, who teaches the creation courses at Michigan State. He disagrees with those who call his courses a violation of the constitutional provision for separation of church and state. And he and his supporters hold it would violate the principle of academic freedom to ban the Bible story of creation.

Professor Moore says that he eschews the teaching of religious doctrine, but stresses the argument that there "must have been a prime mover" behind creation. Things all around us are too complicated and precise in their design to have evolved that way by accident.

If you still doubt, I have some suggestions.

Try to find an explanation for this thing called "life."

If oak trees grow from acorns, where did the first acorn come from?

Or look at a common, ordinary steel girder—the kind that supports the tremendous weight of our office skyscrapers. It looks solid and strong. Well, it's strong, all right, but scientists tell us it's *not solid*.

A steel girder, they have found, actually is composed of a mass of electrons that whirl around each other at an incredible—but very precise—speed. Take sample after sample. Researchers say the whirling and the speed will be precisely the same.

You and I can't possibly see this wonder of nature. But I haven't heard of anyone arguing that it's a lie.

Science tells us the same precision and uniformity of movement is found in the minute particles of every substance on earth. And the same precision applies to the timing of movements of the planets and stars.

Or, again, look at the wonders performed by this strange power called electricity. When scientists learned the laws that govern it, they converted it into one of man's greatest servants. Before that, it was a menace that burned houses and barns in every thunderstorm.

Obey the laws that control electricity and it will give us light, heat, power, music and instant communication across the earth. Ignore them and you will die in a flash.

These so-called "wonders of science" are not being *created* by our scientists, they are being *discovered*. Obviously, they were put there by a super-intelligence. Let's call it God.

To me it seemed poetically fitting that when man first sent one of his man-made machines into orbit around the moon, the first words spoken in space at that great moment were words of praise for the Creator.

And remember, those words were spoken by a man of science.

Indeed, the theologians owe a debt of gratitude to the men of science. For it is the scientist who has proved the existence of God in the most concrete and understandable terms.

And the deeper the men of science delve into the mysteries still hidden in the earth, the deeper the conviction that someone far more intelligent and powerful was here before us.

Now that science has progressed so far that it has found the means to destroy this whole magnificent creation, the work of those of us in the spiritual realm becomes more urgent.

The pace of our work must be speeded. The secret of inner transformation must be made known to many millions, and quickly, for we face the ultimate folly of self-destruction.

The place to start is here and now—with *you*.

If you and other millions like you accept this secret the course of history can be altered.

There must be a special effort to win the support of our leaders, and to win the hearts and minds of the practitioners of evil in our society.

And this is happening.

A prominent United States Senator—a man so admired in his home state that he was assured of long continuance in office—resigned his seat in the Senate. He has dedicated the rest of his life to working among leaders of the country and bringing as many as he can to accept this great transforming secret.

His name is Harold Hughes, of the state of Iowa.

While we read in the papers only of the troubles and the scandals on Capitol Hill, there are scores of men and women in both houses of the Congress who meet regularly and privately to speed the cause of spiritual transformation among our leaders.

The President of the United States, Jimmy Carter, is the most outspoken of our transformed leaders, but he is only one of a growing number.

Mankind has a built-in sense of the existence of God.

Men may deny it with words, but the very complexity of the minds of those who deny their Creator is one of the most convincing proofs that their denials are false.

I lived for more than two decades in an underdeveloped pagan country. I took part in the primitive superstitious worship of that land. I can testify that even the most backward villagers, who have never seen the wonders of the modern world, are acutely conscious of an all-knowing, higher Power.

Their moral ethics may be crude. But their faith that there is a great Spirit of the universe is solid.

In every village you will find a shrine to the "unknown God." Though they may identify their vague deity by different names, they all make it clear that it is HE, this unknown being who is the force behind everything that exists.

Perhaps you never thought of the Bible as a history book in reverse; a history book written in advance of history. But that is essentially what it is. It is the accurate prophecies of the Bible, prophecies fulfilled centuries later, that give it the authentic feel of a work inspired by a higher intelligence.

It would be childish to brush aside this accurate charting of events, centuries before they happened, as just "good guessing" by the ancient prophets.

For instance, did you know that the birth of Jesus Christ, His suffering and His death were foretold by the prophet Isaiah seven hundred years before Jesus was actually born?

The prophet's story of Jesus reads so much like an eyewitness account that many who hear it read in the churches mistake it for one of the New Testament accounts that were all written shortly after His death.

You will find this amazing prophecy in the book of Isaiah.

But this is only one of countless prophecies and insights that have labeled the Bible as the Word of God and have kept it on the best-seller lists for many thousands of years.

If all this evidence still leaves you cold and unconvinced, there is still another question I want you to think about.

Is it likely that all of the hundreds of millions of devout believers are deliberately lying to you when they describe the transformation that has been wrought in their lives?

Isn't it likely that some smart skeptic would have exposed it as a hoax by now?

If the secret we are talking about did not, in fact, exist, is it plausible that, as a mere fable, it would have been passed down from generation to generation through the centuries?

You know that there are millions of people who publicly testify that the power of God has transformed their lives. May I remind you that testimony of this kind is being accepted as truth every day in our courts of law?

One of the tragedies of our day is that so many of our youth ignore what is available here so readily, and at the same time admit that inner transformation is what they are searching for.

Tens of thousands have taken the detour into Eastern mysticism, eagerly hoping it will so stimulate their minds and souls that they will come into close touch with their Creator.

They believe, quite correctly, that when they get in touch with the Source of life they will live in the divine current. But they are complicating their search. The God they are looking for is offering what they want, quite openly and freely.

So many of them have the order of things reversed.

They have taken the word of the philosophers of humanism that they must first go through a rigid discipline to make themselves moral and acceptable in every way. And only then, they think, can they seek a personal contact with God.

The true way is exactly the opposite.

Seek first a contact with the living God.

Morality, integrity, joyful fulfillment and all the other good things will follow.

I hope I have made my case. I hope you are now prepared to concede there must be an all-powerful God, and that He is the Creator of everything that exists.

Now maybe you still think you are not the type of person that such a God would want to have as a friend.

Well, you are at least partly correct. You don't deserve what God is offering. But He forgives you for your failures, and He wants you to have it anyway.

Thousands, every day, are humbly reaching out and accepting this gift they don't deserve.

They, and the millions who have gone before them, have been astounded at the change that surrender and acceptance bring to their lives.

Suddenly, the earth becomes a happy place!

Everything, in some mysterious way, seems different!

This shoddy world becomes a place of excitement and challenge!

Your eyes seem to play tricks on you. You look at people you used to dislike, or even hate, and you feel your heart swelling with compassion and love for them! It seems impossible! But there it is!

You feel an urge to sing and even to shout in happiness!

You were lonely, possibly isolated, but now everywhere you look you see friendly faces!

The conscience which has worked so hard to get your attention is silent and at rest!

This is unbelievable! But there is more.

As a "bonus," now that you are no longer a fugitive from the laws of God and nature, you have the limitless privilege of private and personal access to the living God himself!

Now just one more question:

Do you want this to happen to you?

Yes?

Then just ask for it right where you are. You don't have to wait till Sunday, or wait till you're in church.

The almighty One himself challenges you to act right now!

6

What We Know about Him

Just about everybody believes there is a God—even those who say they don't believe it.

The inborn sense that there is an all-powerful Creator is standard equipment in the human make-up. In most people, most of the time, it lies dormant, deep in the subconscious. But it leaps into the conscious within a split second in the face of crisis.

I cannot count the number of times I have heard a hardened nonbeliever cry out to God for help at the bedside of a dying child, or when his own life hangs in the balance.

If all else fails, even the confirmed atheist has been known to give God a try. The inborn sense of God overrules the negative argument of the mind in the face of mortal danger.

Of course, when everything is going well, our atheist friends will stoutly defend their thesis that God is a myth.

Just one rung up the ladder from the

bottom, where the atheist stands, is the stubborn "agnostic." He is the kind who just sits on the fence and refuses to argue or to think. He only shakes his head and insists he doesn't know anything about any God, and that there's no way he or anybody else can find out.

Some of these have been known to move just a fraction farther in the direction of belief. They concede that they "hope" there is a God, and that if it turns out there really is one, they would like Him to be friendly.

There aren't very many real atheists. It's such an empty, negative philosophy that few persons of intelligence find any satisfaction defending it. One of the truest bits of discovery that came out of World War II was put into words by a nameless chaplain in a letter home. He wrote: "There are no atheists in the foxholes."

But "agnostics" seem to be legion. So I think I should, for their sake, sound this warning, drawn from my own experience: When an agnostic gets into trouble as the result of breaking the laws of God, he will find that he is in *double trouble*. The reason should be plain. Before he can get help in his trouble from a God who wants to give it, he's got to find faith that God exists. Only then can he expect to get help in finding the way out of whatever mess he's gotten himself into.

I have talked and agonized with some who were in that fix. I remember one, in particular—a young man just home from a tour of service overseas for one of the departments of the federal government.

Like many other single youths he had led a rather wild life when he was abroad. He had sampled just about every physical pleasure in the books. But this young man was blessed with an unusually forceful conscience. And by the time he came to see me he was so crushed in spirit by the memories of his loose life style that he wept like a child. He begged me to pray and intercede for him with "my" God, and ask Him to wipe out the nightmarish memories that were torturing him.

This was the opening I had hoped for. I pointed out to him that if "my" God could help *him,* then "my" God must also be *his* God.

In his desperation he said: "I don't know who to pray to or how to pray, and I'm afraid to try. You will have to do it for me. I want to wipe out the past and start over again. I just can't live with myself as I am now."

Exhausted, he fell silent, and I began quietly to explain to him that he had already prayed without knowing it, when he said he wanted to wipe out the past and start over again.

"God certainly knows by now that you are sincere, and He has given us His word that He will do what we ask if we ask with the kind of honesty and sincerity you have shown.

"There is no 'police record' in God's books. Your past is forgotten. Just believe that your

Creator loves you, and follow the guidance of that wonderful conscience He gave you. You have a great new life right now, starting this moment!"

He gave me the wide-eyed, puzzled look of one who wants desperately to believe what he is hearing.

"But people will remember, they will talk—" he began.

"There's a whole new world of friends out there who know nothing of you before today," I told him. "And they won't 'talk.' "

As I spoke, I looked out the door of my office and saw one of the youth leaders of the church coming toward us. "Here's one of your new friends now," I added. "Jim, come on in here and meet Tom. I think he'd enjoy meeting some of the others."

One of the toughest obstacles to remove from the road to full acceptance of the power of God in the life of the individual is, strangely, a "fear" of God.

So many Americans seem to have the notion that the Creator is a vicious despot whose joy is to punish them for whatever they have done wrong.

Thus, they expect the worst to happen if they come clean and confess their crimes against nature and against God. So they try every detour known to man—everything except honest confession of what they have done, and a humble request to be forgiven.

And while they waste weeks and years on this futile search for an "easy way" out of their trouble, they just sink deeper and deeper into it. And they tend to become superstitious—they begin to look upon every illness, every minor accident or every major tragedy as punishment from God. Even worse, they pass on these distorted views of the ways of the almighty One to their children. And in this there may be the danger of a new paganism growing up right here in this land of enlightenment.

The most urgent message any counselor can give is that the right way, the only way, to escape from the torture of spiritual and physical trouble is "*the easy way*," because God is a loving God, not an angry God. He asks only that you repent of your violations of God's laws and let Him know that you want Him to transform your life in the way He has promised.

It is sad, but true, that many suffering people find this hard to believe, so they go right on suffering.

I am keenly aware of the "fear factor" that robs so many of the gifts God wants to give them, because I was a Buddhist until the age of seventeen. Fear is built into the Buddhist belief that the Creator will surely punish you for sins in this life by sending you back to this world in the next life as one of the lower animals.

I escaped from the tortures of this ghastly belief when I learned that God is a loving father, not an angry judge. I abandoned Buddhism and was rocketed into a new life of deep fulfillment on a surge of great joy. And it has been happy all the way.

With this in my own background I feel an urgent duty to tell the tortured ones who are suffering memories of immorality, dishonesty, violence and other violations of God's law: "There is no punishment! God wants to forgive you and forget your past! You can start a new life today! The transformation is free, compliments of your Creator."

God is not in the business of manufacturing human beings and then refusing to stand behind His product. When the human element breaks down, there is always the divine repairman ready to provide new parts by the miracle of inner transformation.

Everything we know of the character of almighty God we have learned in two ways: from the Bible—the authenticity of which I will talk about later—and from His transformation of human beings, which we see happening around us every day, if we look for it.

Let's look at some of the descriptions of His character handed down to us over many thousands of years in the Bible.

Over and over again, He is described as a shepherd. Now the modern American doesn't often have a chance to watch a shepherd, but I have traveled to the Middle East many times, so let me suggest what this shepherding business means.

God and His angels are like a good shepherd and his wonderfully expert shepherd dogs. The shepherd and his canine helpers know their way through the dry desert areas. They can find water holes in the driest regions.

The constantly moving dogs, in their protective rounds, sense the presence of predatory animals and give chase before the sheep know they are there. When a dog barks to warn the shepherd that a lamb has grown tired and fallen behind, the shepherd picks it up and carries it awhile.

The shepherd doesn't quit work and go home at five p.m. So long as his flock is out in the open, so is he. At night he finds the shelter of a cave for his sheep, and he makes his bed across the entrance to protect them.

God, the Shepherd, has on occasion, saved me from death or injury.

A few weeks ago, during a winter storm, my car went out of control on an icy bridge. As it spun, I saw that it was headed for collision with the railing, and possibly for a fall into the water.

"Help me, God," I breathed. And even while I was speaking the words, help came. The car miraculously came out of the spin and made a neat U-turn without any help from me. Then it gently rolled to a stop at the side of the road. I sat there a few moments to steady my nerves and to say a few words of thanks before driving on.

And here is another case of very clear divine intervention:

I know a young businessman who was suddenly paralyzed, and for days had been suffering pain that seemed almost unbearable.

With other friends I went to his home to do what I could for him. "Have you asked God to relieve you of this pain?" I inquired. Gritting his teeth and groaning, he shook his head.

"Then why don't we do that right now?" I suggested. And, with the other friends gathered around him, we spoke to God in the conversational tones we begin to use when we get well-acquainted with Him. We told Him how concerned we were for our friend, and we assured Him of our faith that He has the power to end this suffering, if it is His will.

As the prayer ended, I noticed that our friend seemed more relaxed than before. "How do you feel now?" I asked.

He gave me a strange look of mingled disbelief and joy. Then he moved one arm, and next the other. He sat up, and with the help of friends he finally stood up, and began to walk up and down the room, swinging his arms and laughing and weeping at the same time.

"He has done it! He has done it!" he shouted. "Oh, thank you, Lord, thank you, thank you!"

Before leaving, we knelt again, to say "thank you."

The Bible also speaks of God as the provider of all good things, and ruler of the universe, Creator and general manager of this world, and the just and fair judge of all that goes on here.

I think God's role as judge may be one of the most widely misunderstood facts of life on earth. Here's an example of how He works:

I have a temper, and it gets out of hand now and then. I know it's wrong to allow that to happen. It's a clear violation of God's law governing human relationships. But it continues to happen.

Now if I should allow this anger to smoulder and build up lasting resentments I'd be on the way to real, deep trouble and even more serious violations of God's laws.

So God, working through my conscience, gives me a gentle warning. And after I've pleaded "guilty" and humbly asked to be forgiven, He lets me off. The only real punishment is a lingering sense of regret that it ever happened.

But if I get stubborn and refuse to admit my guilt, and let my anger develop into hatred; if I move on to still greater sin by spreading gossip about the one who is the target of my hatred, the divine Judge begins to punish me while these spiritual crimes are still building up. The punishment starts gradually and is intensified, step by step.

At first, my relations with people around me

start to deteriorate. The joy drains out of my life. I find it, at first, difficult, and later impossible to do the work I have enjoyed for so many years. If my stubbornness persists, I may even lose my job. All because I have let a temper tantrum get out of control!

The pressure of punishment continues to grow, and so does my inner misery. And finally, at long last, the message gets through the poisonous anger that has distorted my thinking.

It dawns on me that God himself has been deliberately making me miserable because He wants me to come to my senses, put in a humble "guilty" plea, accept His forgiveness and end this stupid, stubborn temper storm.

That is the way God-the-judge does His work. He invokes punishment gradually, increasing pressure until the criminal halts the crime.

And when the spiritual crime is halted, He is quick to forgive.

But He leaves you with a vivid memory of your folly, and of the misery and heartache it caused. That remains as a warning against making the same mistake again.

7

Does Prayer Do Any Good?

There's a prosperous businessman in a large eastern city who tells this story of what prayer did for him:

"It saved my truck-leasing business from underworld racketeers," he says, "and it saved my life in the bargain.

"I was just getting started and was worried sick by bills. On one of my worst days I was approached by a well-known underworld figure. He wanted a half-dozen of my trucks, but even in the midst of my financial worries I shied away from him—that is, I did until I heard his offer. It was fantastic!

"I knew the risks of dealing with this man, I knew the danger of the underworld getting control of both my affairs and myself. But I also knew that my books were foreshadowing financial failure. So I quieted my conscience, took a deep breath, and said 'yes.'

"The money rolled in from this shady

customer, but I noticed that many other customers rolled out and never came back.

"My nerves got jumpy, as my only customer took out more and more of my vehicles. I knew it was illegal work. I lay awake at night. I expected the police to call and tell me they had seized my trucks. 'If they get caught, I'm finished,' I thought. 'Why did I ever let myself into this one-crooked-customer deal?'

"Then one night when I was tossing in my bed, I turned on the bed lamp and reached out for a book. What I picked up was the Bible. And it opened at once, as if on order, to the book of Ecclesiastes.

"As I peered through reddened, tired eyes at the printed page I came into focus on the second verse of the eleventh chapter. And I read: 'Put your investments in several places—many places even—because you never know what kind of bad luck you are going to have in this world.'

"I began to sweat! This, it seemed certain, was a message addressed directly to me. It must be! God himself is speaking to me. I must find a way to speak to Him," I said to myself.

"So I knelt by the bed and wept out my bitterness and my fears and my deep regret at having so grossly violated God's law. I don't remember saying anything, except, possibly, 'I'm so sorry, God. Please help me.'

"And suddenly, as I knelt there in the early hours of the morning, my heart was flooded with a warm, comfortable feeling of contentment and happiness. It was overpowering! In my whole long life as a nominal believer, it was my first real contact with God, the giver of life!

"I saw in a flash how foolish I had been to allow myself to be trapped into an immoral, crooked business deal in my lust for money. And I heard myself telling God I would break off the whole deal the next day. And then perhaps I fainted, or slept, because all I can remember is a feeling of relief, of freedom, of deep satisfaction and happiness—and the feeling stayed with me and was still giving me courage when I awoke from a restful sleep the next morning.

"I went straight to my office, telephoned my only customer, and told him to bring back my trucks and take his business elsewhere.

"He was furious, of course, and he suggested plainly that I had better have some 'good protection' because unprotected trucks quite often are stolen or damaged.

"I assured him in a voice ringing with confidence that I was in touch with the finest protection you could get in this world, and suggested it might not be wise to try anything rough. We parted bitter enemies. But I felt no fear.

"And it was then that the miracles began to happen!

"As I hung up the telephone, it rang again. A

brand new customer wanted a half-dozen trucks the next day!

"Other calls poured in. I had to borrow vehicles from a competitor who was glad to lend them because he had little business. Competitors, who knew of the trap I had been caught in, began to call and make discreet attempts to find out what happened.

"I told them, frankly and truthfully, that I had contacted the living, loving God of creation for the first time in my life! And they laughed heartily and thought I was joking."

That is the whole story as he told it to me, because he knew I would not laugh.

His business has prospered in the years since that incident, and his anti-racket protection—"the best you could get in this world"—has never failed.

I know that story is true, because I have been personally very close to the man who told it. His story should make clear that prayer can be a very practical tool in everyday life. It is not just a ritual to be repeated when you are in church.

And here is another example of practical results from prayer—another story that I can guarantee is true because I watched it happen:

A conscientious student with a brilliant mind was having an intensive struggle to stay in college because of an extreme nervous tension. Though he studied long and late, he failed one examination after another. Always he blamed himself, and he penalized himself for being "such an idiot," when he was sure, in his less nervous moments, that he knew his subject backward and forward.

But things got worse and worse. The school authorities knew he was a bright youth, but they were on the point of telling him he had to leave the school because they simply could not "fake" passing grades for him when he so consistently failed in his examinations.

He came to talk to me one day, in a state of deep depression. And when he had poured out the story I told him the problem he faced was very simple to solve.

"All you have to do," I suggested, "is place yourself completely in the hands of God, and," I added, "quit trying to force yourself to memorize the details of everything that He has created."

So he began a program of daily prayer. He prayed before he studied, and again afterward. He told the Lord that if He would cooperate with him, if He would handle his nervousness at the next exam, he—the youth—would be able to handle the exam itself.

I saw him almost daily as the new routine progressed. His very appearance changed. He began to open up and blossom like a bud in the spring. His face radiated health and happiness. He looked and acted like a man who hadn't a care in the world.

His school mates began to repeat to each other the joking remarks that he began to make, extemporaneously and apparently without effort. He began to gain a reputation as a "wit" and a pleasant fellow to be with.

He continued to study hard, but no longer was he a slave to his books. And at last came the showdown week of examinations. To fail this time was the end.

He tackled every question with enthusiasm. He told me later that there was such joy in his heart that he almost laughed out loud right in the midst of the tests.

And when it was over: He had passed everything "with distinction"!

The atheists may scoff, and the agnostics may doubt, but the testimony and the facts in this case are documented in the school records.

In recent years I have been puzzled and somewhat appalled by the headlong rush of so many Americans to delve into the secrets of the Oriental mystic religions.

I am, of course, an Oriental myself—a Chinese by birthright and a Javanese national by birth, now an American citizen by choice.

As a graduate student in a seminary I wrote a thesis on Eastern mysticism, so I can understand the appeal of these man-made philosophies that are tailored to appeal to troubled Western minds.

But I still find it ironic that in the Western world, so advanced in its Christian orientation, the "in thing" has become a search for aid in understanding divine intervention by devouring the books written by Oriental mystics.

It is a racket—nothing less.

The owners of book shops are making fortunes selling literally tons of paperback volumes expounding the Eastern mystic theories of the relationship between the divine and the human. The "gurus" are making a financial "killing," too.

They all recognize the existence of God, of course. But they call Him by many different names, and they assign to Him many different, and some peculiar, powers.

Personally, I am convinced that many of these Oriental gurus are a lot smarter than our Western theologians, in at least one way: they have studied their market. They know the inner longings of the "seekers after truth" who come to them. And they model their various gods to suit the imaginings of their more sophisticated followers.

For example, one of the more widely accepted models of Oriental gods is one who is introduced as "the principle of the human soul." Because he is part and parcel of the human soul, they say, he is reachable by the human race.

It is tragic that there are so many people today who blithely acknowledge their ignorance of God, but are too proud to listen to anyone who wants to talk intelligently about

Him. It is no wonder they shrink back at the idea of speaking directly to God by the act we call "prayer." That, they insist, is oversimplification. Contact with the Supreme Being, they say, could not be made that simply. But the truth is, they are *overcomplicating* the process and thus are missing one of life's most rewarding experiences.

I have prayed many times every day of my life, ever since my life was transformed by a reading of Paul's letter to the Romans, at the age of seventeen. I was a Buddhist one moment, and a transformed, deliriously joyous Christian a moment later. So let me try to "walk you" through the initial contact with almighty God, and tell you what may happen to you.

At the very instant that you know your soul has at last contacted the source of life, God himself, your mind rises above the clutter of your physical surroundings. You become acutely and intensely aware that you have made contact with the Power of a new world.

You feel an overwhelming urge to open your very soul and unload every thought, every problem and every burden, as this marvelous presence invites you to do.

Don't be surprised if, at this moment, you melt into tears of both sorrow and joy.

Your mind seems more sharp and clear than ever before. You are able, suddenly, to convert the deepest desires of your heart into thoughtful, relaxing prayer.

You feel no reticence in asking for something—or everything—you think you really need. But you hear yourself making these requests in a polite and considerate manner. You preface or follow every request with the humble proviso: "if it is your will," or "if it pleases you."

Finally, when this initial contact is concluded, you will experience a feeling of absolute confidence that His power and His presence are in you and around you.

The sudden change in you, personally, will be noticed by friends and family.

You will suddenly come to life. You will find a new enthusiasm, new encouragement and a new and abundant energy. Your outlook will be positive and optimistic, and there will be no clouds to temper it.

Everything around you probably will remain the same, but to you it will all seem new and exciting. The truth is that the only real change that has been made is *the change in YOU*.

Every human who meets the living God comes out of that experience permanently changed.

Now, back to the original question: "Does prayer do any good?"

The answer, I think, has been given by the stories and the discussion in this chapter. Obviously, prayer can change things for the good.

But perhaps we should ask, also: "What *is* prayer?"

"Prayer" is simply a theological word indicating a contact or conversation with God.

Prayer could become a greater factor in both personal and public affairs if everyone understood that it is *not* something you have to do *to please God*; it is something you do for the edification of *your own soul*.

It is not something you do because you are required to do it; a prayer is the reaction to a personal need or a reaction of thankfulness to a loving God for his favors.

It is too bad that so many professing believers think they can pray properly only in church or in presence of a priest or a preacher. So many seem to have the notion that unless some professed Christian is kneeling or sitting with them, with closed eyes, their desires or requests will not be heard or fulfilled.

Look at it this way: A child does not need someone to help him make a request to his parents. God is your father.

What matters to Him is not the wording of your prayer, but what is in your heart.

You don't need any human help to rise up closer to God, because He is willing and able to come down and get closer to *you*.

All these things I know to be true because I have experienced them all myself.

8

A Vacuum to Fill

One of the first things I learned in the basic science course in high school was that nature simply cannot tolerate a vacuum.

Remove something—anything—from the space it occupies, and something else is going to fill that space immediately, even if it's only air.

That is one of the absolute laws that govern things as they are in this world.

Years later, when I began to study spiritual things, I ran into the same law again.

I learned that when God transforms the life of one who seeks Him, all the rebellious violations of God's law are removed, and they are replaced by a spiritual urge to do what is right and good.

But there is still a spiritual vacuum within the transformed person. He wants to do the right things, but he's new in this field. He needs help to find the kinds of activity in this new life that will take the place of the old habits that were discarded. Only then will the vacuum be filled, and a source of possible error removed.

To give this early guidance is a grave responsibility. If you are new in the faith your best source of counsel is your pastor. But do not hesitate to ask advice of those around you who display the glow of happy lives. They are eager to help.

All who are experienced in the faith have traveled the same road. They understand your problem. And what is more, they know the anguish and guilt that they would feel if any advice they gave, or anything they did or did not do, should cause a new believer to stumble into error. They will not give advice lightly.

In nature, vacuums are filled automatically.

Try it out. Light your fireplace some cold winter day. As the flames rise high a greater and greater volume of hot air goes up the chimney. Then you will sense another movement of air. Cold drafts from the outside will start whistling through every tiny crack and crevice of your home. That hot air going up your chimney has got to be replaced. The vacuum has to be filled. Outside air has to come in.

In spiritual things, the same kind of balance is maintained in the discarding of old ways and the taking on of the new.

If you were an active leader among the sinners in your old life, you're almost certain to be an active leader among the believers after

God performs His miracle of transformation.

To aim at the same degree of activity in the new life, as in the old, is a good way to be sure you haven't overlooked any unfilled vacuums.

Remember the dramatic transformation of the apostle Paul? He was the chief among the persecutors of the early church until that day on the Damascus Road. Then God transformed him into the chief among leaders of the early church.

Similar miracles are happening today.

A leading political criminal of Watergate is now the enthusiastic leader of a nationwide prison ministry. He and the group around him are working to bring hope and life-transforming power to wasted lives behind the walls.

New believers are just about unanimous when you ask them what was their most unforgettable experience when they first encountered the living God.

"It was the sense of relief, the freedom from anxiety and worry. It was the feeling that a heavy weight of excess baggage had been lifted from tired shoulders."

God's medicine and man's seem to operate on the same principle. Medical men try to give their patients, at the very first, the same feeling of relief and confidence.

The first thing an ambulance doctor does for an accident victim is loosen his tie, put a rolled-up coat under his head, and ask him if he is comfortable. Then, in his most confident voice, he tells the unhappy victim that "everything's going to be all right."

When man approaches God in true humility confessing guilt, he gets, first, a strong, positive assurance that "all is forgiven, and—even more—forgotten." Only then comes that thrilling, painless operation that makes him a new man, and gives this shoddy world a new aura of excitement.

To you it may sound too self-evident to be mentioned, but it is important that new believers know God intends to keep them busy. It must have been some homespun philosopher who summed up the reason for the Creator's concern for His people's working schedule in the old, but accurate, saying: "An idle mind is the devil's workshop."

In case you think work—real fruitful activity—is not properly a part of the spiritual life, remember this: God's people, in comparison with the world's total population, are a very small minority. We are so small, in fact, that every man and woman is needed to obey God's command to spread the Word to all the world.

An epidemic of idle minds in the camp of the believers is exactly what the forces of evil need.

Work and the planning of work is always uppermost in the divine plan for those who serve Him.

Centuries before you were born, the Bible tells us, God knew that you were going to be born. He also knew when and where, and well in advance of that date He had plotted the course of your whole life.

The Creator went to a lot of trouble to see to it that your life would be successful, fulfilling and zestful. If it isn't, then you've made a wrong turn somewhere along the route that was plotted. If this is, indeed, the way it is with you, it's time for you to get on your knees and ask Him for another look at the road map.

Cultivation of the mind is an important part of the duty of every Christian.

I feel it is a tragedy that so many of us neglect this duty.

Even worse, there are some among us who have convinced themselves the mind is the primary source of evil, and that too much thinking, therefore, leads to sin.

Some go so far as to limit the amount of schooling they allow their children, in order to protect them from pollution of the mind.

The complex mind of man is one of the most staggering wonders of God's creation. Every detail of everything that touches his life is screened by it, filtered through it, and channelled by it for action or discard.

The mind is the seat of consciousness. It is the communications channel that conscience uses to guide our moral and spiritual attitudes.

It is, in addition, the primary tool in all our work.

Regretfully, the mind is also the part of our make-up that is most accessible to temptation. That, probably, is what has given the wonderful human brain a bad reputation among certain groups of sincere believers. I, myself, am convinced these good people have vastly overemphasized its dangers, and underestimated its potential for good.

The mind of man, in truth, is a lot like a modern computer. What comes out of it depends entirely on the quality of what goes in. As the computer programmers put it: "Garbage in; garbage out."

Remember, the mind is a gift from God. And who among us—having surveyed the wonders that have flowed from the minds of humans in this century of civilization—would dare to face the almighty One and tell Him He made a mistake in giving us the power to learn, to reason and to think?

Before we get too far away from the discussion of the mind, let's look for a moment at another item that is closely related to it; let's look for a moment at the nature, and the sources, of "truth."

Exactly what is "truth"?

I think most philosophers agree that "truth," in essence, is *reality*.

Now "reality," in layman's language, means

"things as they are" or "telling it like it is." Reality is the sum total of the orderly laws of God and nature, designed by God to keep the stars and planets in their orbits, to keep the earth in its proper relation to the sun, so that we neither burn up nor freeze, and to keep all the other activities on this globe moving smoothly and free from disastrous collisions or tangles.

That is "reality" as we find it in nature, and as we see it daily. But there is another way to determine the nature of reality. When God gave the earth to mankind to operate and manage, he also handed us an operating manual. That was many thousands of years ago.

At some time in the distant past it became known as the Holy Bible. The very fact that it has been preserved and passed down through the centuries is evidence enough of its supernatural origin.

But there is more specific evidence that this book indeed is the ultimate source of truth.

The friends of God, the believers—most recently, the Christians—have been alerted, in advance, of coming events in history for centuries by careful reading of the prophecies of this great book.

In the Dark Ages, the truth contained in the Bible was the force that preserved civilization.

It has always been a delight and a comfort to the friends of God, and a source of confounding amazement to those who do not believe.

Several years ago I was a firsthand witness to an incident in a non-Christian, foreign land that underlined the power of this holy book.

A group of anti-Christian zealots in that country organized a widespread research project that was aimed specifically at discrediting the Bible. It was headed by a brilliant young scholar with whom I was acquainted.

The plan was to focus on the "many errors" in the Bible and then to publish a detailed exposé that would demonstrate beyond doubt that, as a work of divine inspiration, it was a fake.

There was a lot of excitement in the papers, and a lot of argument back and forth between believers and zealots. Weeks went by, then month after month passed, and the researchers failed to surface.

Finally the announcement did come. There was to be a press conference. The results of the study would be told.

The auditorium was packed on the appointed day. Reporters were there en masse. They scented a "big story."

Finally, my friend, the brilliant young scholar walked onto the platform, and a hush fell over the crowd. They had noted that he had no papers with him. There was no sign of a report.

"I have completed my study," he said, "and I

have come here to report that it did not go according to plan.

"I have to say that I have been unable to establish the proof of error I expected to find. This was true in our studies of both the Old Testament and the New."

Then, as the room buzzed with surprise, he dropped a bombshell:

"I must tell you, frankly," he said, "that my studies have convinced me the Bible is, indeed, a work that was truly inspired by some mysterious higher power.

"As for me, I intend to continue the study, and to look at this book seriously and sympathetically. I cannot, honestly, approach it now as an antagonist."

This whole project had been given the official support of the government of that country. You can imagine the sensation that its reverse outcome produced in the press and among the nonbelieving population.

Every time I think of that exciting day I am reminded that the same thing had happened before, in another country, some two thousand years ago.

The young researcher was a modern Saul of Tarsus, who battled against the truth, but finally embraced it after it had utterly defeated him.

Over the centuries there have been impressive testimonials to the accuracy and value of the Bible.

A poet and singer called David, who later became the King of Israel, was inspired to put his testimony into verse. He wrote:

"It revives my soul."

"It gives wisdom to those who lack it."

"It rejoices my heart."

"It enlightens my eyes."

"It is more desirable than the finest gold."

"It is sweeter than the purest honey."

If there is any vacuum in your life, the Bible can show you how to fill it.

Quite apart from the factual truth in its pages, the Holy Bible has been admired by the scholars of many generations as easy-to-read literature that contains so many hidden truths it can bear repeated readings.

Taken as a whole, the Bible is, indeed, a simply-written, straightforward description of the secret of zestful living, and it applies to any period of the thousands of years of history through which it has existed.

One of the most persuasive proofs that the Bible is holy writ is the accuracy of its prophecies.

Two thousand seven hundred years ago—700 years before the birth of Jesus Christ—the ancient prophet Isaiah told of the forthcoming birth of Jesus in a prophecy recorded in the book of Isaiah.

Not only His birth was predicted in that account, but also His suffering and death at the hands of His own people.

These were events that did not happen until 700 years later. But if you read the 700-year-old prophecy in the light of what actually happened, it sounds like an account prepared by one who had witnessed, firsthand, these events which were still so far in the future when it was written.

The arrival of Jesus on earth, His death and resurrection revolutionized the spiritual life of all mankind.

The picture of God the father as a stern judge and dispenser of punishment was changed. Jesus proclaimed that God is the personification of love. No one need suffer punishment for sins, He said, because His death wiped out the sins of every human being who accepts Him and lives by His teachings.

Worship of God became a matter of joy instead of fear.

To the curious who gathered to hear Him speak, His invitation was always the same; always aimed at the tired and the troubled: "Come unto ME all ye who are weary and heavy laden, and I will give you rest." He came across as a genuinely warm human being.

There is no question that Jesus was an historical figure. Even the non-Christian historians acknowledge that the closely paralleled accounts of His life and work, written by authors at different times and places, leave no doubt on this score.

That His mission was successful is also witnessed by history and the historians. The countless millions who follow Him today are still growing in numbers and spreading to new places.

The miracle of Jesus' life and death and resurrection is still—after two thousand years—recognized as THE turning point in all of human history.

What He did on earth and what He offers you, will be covered in the next chapter. But the question "why" he holds His offer open to nonbelievers after two thousand years of waiting can be answered here: It is the measure of God's love.

9

Jesus and You

I know it's not fair for a writer to ask questions of his readers, when he knows he's not going to be there to hear the answer. But I'm going to do it just once more because there's no other way to get my point across.

There's always somebody who scoffs and argues when I declare, as I just did, at the close of the last chapter, that the brief life and sacrificial death of Jesus marked THE turning point in all of human history.

Let's say you disagree. Then why, for the last two thousand years, have we dated our calendars and numbered our years from the time of His birth?

All the events of history now are identified as having happened either "before Christ" or after. If that's not THE turning point of history, then show us another one. If there were a clearer turning point I'm sure someone would have discovered it by now.

But the Christian calendar is not the only—nor even the best—argument for His deity.

Jesus was born poor, and was penniless throughout His life. He never commanded an army. Yet, He alone has conquered many millions more than the armies of Caesar, Alexander, Napoleon and Hitler combined.

Jesus never wrote a single line. But the words He spoke have set in motion more pens and typewriters and printing presses than we can number.

The wisdom He spread so casually among the poor and unschooled of His time has furnished material for more debates, orations, discussions, sermons, books, paintings, sculptures, songs and poems than the thoughts of all the other great men of ancient and modern times.

Without any formal schooling, Jesus shed more light on things human, scientific and divine than all the host of philosophers and scholars of history.

No one who was with Him during His life on earth ever suggested that He was an eloquent speaker, yet the words He spoke have lived longer and had an impact greater than the words of any orator or poet still remembered.

The things Jesus said and the things He promised have never been successfully discredited or questioned in the two thousand years that His sayings and promises have been published and repeated across the world. And what pronouncements and promises they were!

"I am the way, the truth and the life: no man cometh unto the Father, but by me . . ." (John 14:6 KJV).

"I am the resurrection, and the life: he that believeth in me, though he were dead, yet shall he live: And whosoever liveth and believeth in me shall never die" (John 11:25, 26 KJV).

"Heaven and earth shall pass away, but my words shall not pass away. . ." (Matt. 24:35 KJV).

"I am the bread of life: he that cometh to me shall never hunger . . ." (John 6:35 KJV).

"I am the light of the world: he that followeth me shall not walk in darkness, but shall have the light of life . . ." (John 8:12 KJV).

Though His own people rejected Him and killed Him, many Jews have openly voiced their admiration of Him down through the centuries. One of them, the scholar Sholem Asch, is quoted as having said this:

"Jesus Christ is the outstanding personality of all time. No other teacher—Jewish, Christian, Buddhist or Mohammedan—is still a teacher whose teaching is such a guidepost for the world we live in. Other teachers may have something basic for an Oriental, an Arab or an Occidental; but every act and word of Jesus has value for us all. He became the light of the world. Why shouldn't I, a Jew, be proud of that?"

Now let's reason together for a moment.

If God were to visit the earth what would we expect of Him? How about this list:

We would certainly expect Him to be sinless.

We would expect Him to speak only the truth, in the clearest, most authoritative manner, using the most exact and appropriate words.

We would expect Him to display a supernatural power, at least sufficient to convince the unbelievers of His link with the supernatural.

We would expect Him to have power over death and to work provable miracles.

Finally, we would expect His words and acts to have a permanent impact on mankind.

There is no doubt at all, in my mind, that Jesus completely fulfilled all of these expectations. I believe His clear assertion that Jesus and God are one.

Now all of this, from the start of this chapter, is just a prelude to the very brief proposals I am about to make.

If you picked up this book because you are in trouble, because you have violated the laws of God, you now have a fairly clear picture of the character and the power of the God you have sinned against.

If you still are convinced in your mind and heart that you can safely continue sinning against almighty God, you should be warned that things are going to get worse for you before they get better. But if you picked up this book in search of a way out of your trouble and misery, you have found it.

Believe the words of Jesus. Make them a model for the rest of your life. Join His people in their work of spreading His Word. Accept Him as the Son of God. Follow Him. Your life will be transformed beyond your wildest hope.

This is the essence of the secret formula we spoke of in chapter one. No one can know *how* He does it; we only know He *does,* and it works. As we said then, it works *best* when things are at their *worst.* Jesus is noted for His accurate timing. His help and His power are always most readily available when they are most desperately needed. If you are fed up with what you've got, take what He is offering, *now.* What he offers is a happy, zestful, useful, productive life, and the bonus of an everlasting life when this one ends.

Now I want to tell you a story of a strange experience that profoundly influenced me in my decision to become a minister of the gospel of Jesus.

It happened in a large Oriental country, not far from the Indonesian island where I was born.

There was a young man, wealthy, educated and a member of the privileged class. Moreover, his parents were influential. He already had everything that he wanted on this earth, and his family was willing and able to give him more if he asked.

Despite the apparent selfishness of his life, this young man was deeply attached to his mother, extraordinarily so. Suddenly tragedy struck. His beloved mother died, without warning.

Both the son and his father were deeply grieved, but the son much more than the father. The boy was crushed in spirit and completely heartbroken. As preparations for the funeral were being made, he came to a solemn resolve. "I cannot live on this earth without my mother," he said. Suicide, he decided, was the only solution.

So he went to his room and began to write a suicide note to his father. But there he found his anguish redoubled by the thought that his father, of whom he was genuinely fond, would be doubly crushed by the loss of both wife and son.

As he paused in his writing, the pen still in his hand, he thought he felt the presence of another person in the room. He knew he had locked the door. Could someone have come in ahead of him and hidden in a closet?

Suddenly fearful, he swung around to face the intruder. What he saw made his heart stand still, he said in later years.

There, in the middle of the room, was a handsome, middle-aged gentleman, dressed in a long white robe, his silvery gray hair hanging below his shoulders. The man smiled in a gentle, compassionate way and held out his hand.

But the youth was so startled at this vision, or this intrusion, that instead of accepting the outstretched hand, he fell on his face on the floor at the visitor's feet.

He testified later that he heard the man speak these words:

"Don't be distressed. I want you to follow me, for I have a task for you. I am Jesus!"

Before he could respond, or even lift his head, the vision disappeared.

He tried the door. It was still locked. He ran to the window. It was closed and locked, and when he looked out, he saw nothing.

Forgetting his suicide note, he sat down to ponder what had happened.

"Why in the world would Jesus visit me?" he asked. "I'm no Christian. I've hardly ever talked to one." In the faith of his family, Jesus was listed only as one among many ancient sages.

He snatched up his suicide note and rushed out to tell his father what had happened. But the older man was not impressed. He decided his son was mentally unbalanced by his mother's death. He preferred to think that, rather than the only alternative: that his son was about to join the infidels!

Disappointed, the youth sought out a

Christian friend and told him the story. And he was puzzled that his friend acted so casual and even seemed to have expected his visit.

Before the youth left, he was handed a copy of the New Testament. This he read and reread intently. He discovered it was the story of Jesus. And people began to ask him what had happened to him. They told him that his face had become radiant, like the moon. His voice had softened, they said, and he had abandoned his selfish ways and had begun, instead, to help the needy.

So astounding was his conversion to Christianity, that people in this non-Christian town began to flock to the one Christian church to learn the secret. Day after day, the sanctuary overflowed. And hundreds in that town accepted Jesus.

Word was spread overseas about this miracle, and the curious came long distances to see this man they called the "living Jesus."

One Western observer who returned home after a visit reported: "I have Christian parents and I have lived all my life in a Christian land; I have also heard Christian teachings by the most celebrated preachers, but never before have I ever seen anyone actually living the life of Jesus as this handsome young man is doing."

Now that is a true story. I believe that God still works through this kind of miracle in pagan lands where His Word cannot get through in any other way. But that is not the point I want to make.

Notice the way Jesus worked. Just as is recorded in the New Testament, He appeared, in this case, at the very moment of the youth's deepest distress.

He did not scold or try to stop the suicide. He spoke gently and held out a forgiving and compassionate hand, the same hand He had held out to beggars and lepers. He identified himself clearly and unmistakably, by name. And He made clear what He wanted the youth to do. He said: "I want you to follow me, for I have a task for you."

This story was related to me when I was a very young man debating a career in the ministry.

It jolted me tremendously, because I had experienced a similar vision only a short time after my own conversion to Christianity. It happened, in my case, in Java, where I spent the first seventeen years of my life as a Buddhist.

The good that flowed out of that earlier miracle, I believed, was the result of the young man's immediate response. This stiffened my resolve to defy my Buddhist father and become a Christian minister. For I, too, faced disgrace then, in the eyes of my family.

I have told you this story for two reasons:
First, because I want you to know that God is

still working miracles in the pagan lands, just as He did in Bible times. I am convinced that it's happening because it's the only way to break the icy resistance to the Truth.

Second, because I want to alert you to the fact that miracles are happening in America, too. Most of us are too sophisticated to recognize a miracle when we see it. I hope your eyes will be opened.

When Christ was on earth, choosing those who would carry on His work, spreading the gospel when He was gone, He seemed to go out of His way to find "losers." He gathered around Him a motley group of poverty-stricken fishermen, small merchants, a revenue agent who hated his job, lepers, cripples and harlots. None of those closest to Him had any standing in the community when He chose them.

To all He gave the same invitation: "Follow me, and I will make you fishers of men."

In three years of on-the-job training at the feet of Jesus they learned their mission well. At the right moment, He gave them supernatural power, and they demonstrated the wisdom of His choice; they turned the world upside down.

Their names and voices still echo down through the centuries. This motley group, these "losers" who were touched by Jesus, were the first of many millions to have their lives transformed by divine power.

Jesus is still looking for the "losers" of this

world, for those in deepest trouble. His offer, made two thousand years ago, is still available.

The secret of inner peace, freedom from fear and trouble, an outer glow of personality that will attract and influence others, and a zestful, successful life—it's an all-inclusive package that comes with the touch of Jesus.

The price?

All you have to do, He says, is "Follow me."

10

The Guarantee

The contents of this book come to you with a written guarantee.

Every promise, every statement, every warning and prediction made in this book you will find plainly stated in God's own book, the Holy Bible. This biblical backing is our guarantee that what we have said is true. And although thousands of years have passed since all this was written down, the warranty period has not yet expired.

All of the divine offers we have talked about are still open. Their truth and effectiveness have been tested by many satisfied millions. I have tested them myself, and I, too, am happily satisfied.

The Creator knows the quality of what He is offering to you, but He still guarantees you against the loss of anything you may discard in accepting His offer to transform your life. If you are disappointed in what He gives you and wish to return to your old life style, your trouble and misery will be regretfully returned, no questions asked. I should add: This doesn't happen very often.

Now to the guarantee of the things we have been talking about:

1. We began with the flat statement that all kinds of trouble start the same way: with sin; that is, with a violation of God's law.

For the biblical guarantee, look at the fourth verse of the third chapter of First John:

"Whosoever committeth sin transgresseth also the law, for sin [trouble] is the transgression of the law."

2. In God's administration of law, just as in our own courts, ignorance of what the law requires is no excuse. Your conscience knows what's wrong and what's right, and it's there to warn you away from trouble.

Centuries ago, Job—a man who is still cited as the greatest expert in the field of trouble—wrote the following inspired words:

"It is a spirit in a man, the breath of the Almighty, that gives him the instinct to know what the law requires" (Job 32:8).

3. Once we know we have broken the law of God, are we punished? Do we have to go through a course of study or do a lot of good deeds before He forgives us? There's a clear answer:

"If we confess our sins [only confess] God . . . will forgive our sins and cleanse us of all unrighteousness" (1 John 1:9 RSV).

The book of Proverbs underlines this offer to forgive, but adds the warning that you'd better confess everything while you are about it. It says: "He who covers his sins and transgressions will not prosper, but he who confesses and forsakes them will obtain mercy" (Prov. 28:13).

In the 32nd Psalm, God's blanket offer to forgive everyone who will confess all the wrong he has done is put into poetry:

"I acknowledged my sin to the Lord, and I did not hide my iniquity. I said: 'I will confess my transgressions to the Lord'; then the Lord did forgive the guilt of my sin."

This is certainly the most important guarantee the almighty One has handed down. Just confess, and be forgiven.

4. If you have any doubt that God will do all that He has promised without waiting for you to do a lot of good deeds to prove to Him you are worthy, look at this statement from His Word:

". . . God saved us out of kindness and love. . . . It was not because of any good deeds that we ourselves had done, but because of God's own mercy. . . . By His grace we are put right with God, and come into possession of the eternal life we hoped for" (Titus 3:4-7).

5. The secret of God's transforming power is still a secret, and probably always will be, here on earth. But the witnesses who testify throughout the Bible as to "how" it happens and "what" happens, and that it "does indeed" happen are too numerous, and their words are too consistent to disbelieve. And even today we have reliable witnesses that He's still doing it. I am one of them. But look, now, at the guarantees of life-transformation written into the Bible:

The apostle Paul, writing to the Corinthians, probably based these words on his own transformation on the Damascus Road: "When anyone is joined to Christ, he is a new being. The old is gone, the new has come" (2 Cor. 5:17).

There is more detail on this divine operation in the thirty-sixth chapter of Ezekiel: "The Lord has spoken: I will give you a new heart and a new mind. I will take away your stubborn heart of stone and give you an obedient heart. I will put my spirit into you and see to it that you follow my laws and keep all the commands I have given you."

Paul describes the transformation this way in his letter to the Romans: "Let God transform you inwardly by a complete change of your mind. Then you will know the will of God, and what is good and pleasing to Him" (Rom. 12:1,2 TEV).

6. It is made clear in the Bible that once God has performed the miracle of transformation in your life, you should become a constant reader of His guidebook, the Bible, both Old and New Testaments. This will keep you from straying off the road and into new law violations and trouble. Paul, in his second letter to Timothy put it this way:

"All scripture is given by inspiration of God, and is profitable for doctrine, for reproof, for correction, for instruction in righteousness: That the man of God may be perfect, throughly acquainted with all good works" (2 Tim. 3:16,17).

The very first of the Psalms also bears down on the importance of study:

"Happy and healthy are those who find joy in obeying the word of the Lord, and who enjoy studying it, day and night. They are like trees that grow beside a stream, that bear fruit at the right time, and whose leaves do not dry up. They succeed in everything they do."

7. It's hard for some to get it through their minds that the God of all creation can be a personal friend, that He is interested in individuals and what they do and say and think, and in their problems.

If you haven't experienced this personal relationship with God, you are missing a thrilling experience, and one of the most important in life. The Bible is loaded with proof that God wants this kind of friendship with you. The 139th Psalm puts it beautifully:

"Lord, you know everything I do. From far away, you understand all my thoughts. You see me, whether I'm working or resting. You know all my actions. Even before I speak, you know what I'm going to say. You are all around me, on every side. You protect me with your power. Where could I go to escape from you? Where could I get away from your presence?" (TEV)

The prophet Isaiah told the ancient Israelites: "The Lord who created you says: 'Don't be afraid, I will be with you. I have called you by name—you are mine. When you pass through deep waters, I will be with you. Your troubles will not overwhelm you. When you pass through fire, you will not be burned. The hard trials that will come will not hurt you. For I am the Lord your God who will save you."

I once read an account of President Jimmy Carter teaching a Sunday school class. He asked them: "What is there about Christianity that makes it unique among all the religions of the world?" After the class had guessed—and guessed wrong—for a few minutes, the President smilingly raised his hand for silence and gave them this answer: "Of all the religions on earth, Christianity is the only one that offers a close personal relationship with the living God."

8. For some new converts, the idea of "talking to God" is frightening. There's no reason why it should be. There's no hard and fast law about how it has to be done. Just make it a conversation with your eyes open, if that's what you prefer. But make it sincere. God will listen to you. He may not answer in the way you expect, but He WILL hear you.

The fourth chapter of Philippians gives some good tips about prayer:

"Don't worry about anything; instead, pray about everything. Tell God what you need, and don't forget to thank him for his answers. If you do this, you will experience God's peace, which is far more wonderful than the human mind can understand. His peace will keep your thoughts and your heart quiet and at rest, as you trust in Jesus Christ."

In the fourth chapter of James there's a timely warning along with the instructions in prayer:

"You do not have what you want because you do not ask God for it. And when you ask, you do not receive it, because your motives are bad. You are asking for things to use for your own pleasures."

9. People in trouble have told me many times that they doubt there IS a God because He allows too much suffering in this world—especially the suffering that they happen to be involved in.

These people are blinded by their trouble. They take no notice of the wonders around them. The proof of God's existence is clear, both in science and in nature. The poet who wrote the eighth Psalm put the proof in beautiful words:

"When I look at the sky, which you have made, and at the moon and stars, which you have set in their places, what is man that you Oh Lord, think of him; mere man, that you care for him? You have made him inferior only to yourself. You crowned him with glory and honor. You appointed him ruler over everything you made. You placed him over all creation; sheep and cattle, and the wild animals, too; the birds and the fish and the creatures in the seas."

The apostle Paul is less poetic about it, but he strikes the same note of wonder in recognizing the existence of God. He wrote in the first chapter of Romans:

"Ever since God created the world, His invisible power and qualities, both His eternal power and divine nature, have been clearly seen. They are perceived in the things that God has made, so the doubters have no excuse at all!"

And, finally, one of the most beautiful of the Psalms, the nineteenth:

"The heavens declare the glory of God; and the firmament shows His handiwork. Each day announces it to the following day, each night repeats it to the next."

10. For the "weary and the heavy laden," for the troubled who do not yet comprehend the reason for their misery, there is a secret key, a basic truth on which other basic truths are based. Keep it in your heart, and use it to determine, in advance, the wisdom or folly of everything you propose to say or do. It will put you on the road to peace with your fellow men, and that is the road that leads to peace with God. This basic truth can be found in the seventh chapter of Matthew, the twelfth verse:

"Do for others what you want them to do for you; this is the meaning of the laws of God, as taught by the prophets."

All Scripture not denoted as KJV (King James Version), RSV (Revised Standard Version), or TEV (Today's English Version) is the author's paraphrase from the original languages.

If you enjoyed this book may we recommend other best sellers available where paperbacks are sold or use this order form:

Qty.		Price	Total
____	Daughter of Destiny—Kuhlman—Buckingham	$1.95	____
____	Day the Dollar Dies—Cantelon	1.45	____
____	Eldridge Cleaver: Reborn—Oliver	1.95	____
____	Healed of Cancer—Jo Lawson	1.95	____
____	Hustler for the Lord—Larry Jones	1.95	____
____	The Jesus Factor—David Manuel	1.95	____
____	Move That Mountain—Jim Bakker	1.95	____
____	On the Other Side—Ford, Balsiger, Tanner	1.95	____
____	Prison to Praise—Merlin Carothers	1.50	____
____	Run Baby Run—Nicky Cruz	1.50	____
____	Shout It From the Housetops—Pat Robertson	1.95	____
____	The Big 3 Mountain-Movers—Jim Bakker	1.95	____
____	Visions of Jesus—Chet & Lucile Huyssen	1.95	____

Add 10% for *Shipping* ____

Total ____

☐ Send Free Order Form—over 250 titles
☐ Send Free Information about *Logos Journal* Magazine
   Include payment to:
      LIF BOOKS
      Box 191
      Plainfield, NJ 07061

Name _____

Address _____

City _____ State _____

Zip _____